SLEIGHS
THE GENTLE
TRANSPORTATION

Sleighs
The Gentle Transportation

CARLO ITALIANO

TUNDRA BOOKS
Montreal & New York

To my daughter Liana who loves horses, too

Originally published under the title *The sleighs of my childhood/Les traîneaux de mon enfance*
by Tundra Books of Montreal

Printing history
1974 First Canadian bilingual edition, Tundra Books
1974 Metropolitan New York Printers' Award for design and printing quality
1975 Canadian Association of Children's Librarians' Gold Medal— "Best Illustrated Book of the Year"
1975 Chosen by Toronto Public Libraries as one of the Top 100 Canadian Children's Books
1976 Hans Christian Andersen Honor Award, Athens, Greece
1978 UK edition, The Bodley Head Ltd., England
1978 First Canadian and US edition, English only
1978 First paperback edition

ISBN 0-88776-103-8   English language edition, paperback

ISBN 0-88776-105-4   English language edition, hardcover

Printed in Great Britain

SLEIGHS
THE GENTLE
TRANSPORTATION

INTRODUCTION

When I was a boy, I could tell what sleigh was coming to my house—or passing near it—by the sound of its bells. There was always a sleigh bell to be heard, tinkling or jingling, bonging or clunking, sometimes singly and sometimes in chorus. For Montreal in the 1920s and 1930s was the sleigh centre of the world.

We had at least 100 inches of snowfall a winter, and sometimes as much as 150. The snow was not always removed from the streets but simply ploughed to the sides. Sand was used only on the sidewalks—and we wished it wasn't because it spoiled our slides. Streets wide enough for four wagons to get by each other in summer barely allowed two sleighs to pass in winter. Snowbanks, sometimes so high we couldn't see over them, separated the sidewalks from the roadways.

I lived in what was then a wonderful part of Old Montreal, in a pretty tree-lined dead-end street with a children's park. My father and mother had settled in the area when they first came from Italy, and for several years they owned a grocery store. Our street was a great street for sleigh watching. We were between two railway stations, near one of the city's most elegant hotels and within walking distance of two of the largest markets in Canada.

There were very few automobiles. Public transportation was mostly by streetcar, and sleigh drivers had to be careful not to let their runners get caught in streetcar-track switches, called *frogs*. Trucks were gradually replacing sleighs, but the transition was slowed down by World War II, and a few sleighs— like those owned by the milkman, the breadman and the local grocer—were still to be seen in the late 1940s.

I started to draw them almost as soon as I could hold a pencil. I would sit in the window of our house and draw whatever sleighs I saw. When I was not in school or drawing, I was outside bothering the sleigh drivers, hitching rides on the backs of the sleighs or asking questions about the horses.

I particularly liked the farmers. Many of their sleighs were homemade and that made them different to the city sleighs. The farmers arrived on Fridays with their winter supplies for the market: salt pork, dry beans, apples, potatoes, turnips, carrots, and other root crops. Since they stayed overnight, they unhitched their horses—which the older boys would lead up to Mrs Charlebois' livery stable on St Felix Street. The owners paid us a nickel, sometimes as much as seven cents, to do it. They didn't know we would have been glad to do it for nothing.

My mother often took me to Bonsecours Market to help her shop. My father had built me a sled and I nailed a Connors Fish box on it to carry the shopping home. There were nine of us children and my mother always made her own sausages, so she needed a lot of meat. Towards Easter a wonderful thing would happen in the market. The grocers all decorated their horses and sleighs with paper flowers—cut from crêpe paper in blues and yellows and pinks. But spring was a frustrating time for all of us kids who loved horses. Patches of pavement would start showing through the snow and the horses would find the pulling very hard. It was difficult for a driver to know the best time to switch over from sleigh to wagon; some streets might still be snow covered, while intersections might have a bare surface. My friends and I had long talks about how a wagon might be built with both runners and wheels that could be moved up and down depending on whether or not there was snow on the streets. We never did figure out a way to do it.

Then years later, around 1948 I guess it was, one day I saw a sleigh that actually had just that—both wheels and runners—either of which could be put into use depending on the state of the streets. I remember standing and watching it. The great sleigh problem had been solved at last. But by that time there was hardly a sleigh left on the streets to make use of it.

1. The Chip Wagon In winter the chip wagons changed their wheels for sleigh runners, but we still called them 'chip wagons,' never chip sleighs. And although we ate from them the year round, their marvellous french-fried potatoes and steamed hot dogs never tasted so good as in winter. The chip wagons stopped after school at municipal skating rinks, and on Saturdays and Sundays at Fletchers Field where the skiers and tobogganers were out. The chips were served in paper cones, always greasy and always wonderfully warm to the touch. There was vinegar for the chips and mustard and cabbage for the hot dogs. For an extra dime, you could get hot buttered popcorn and roasted peanuts in the shell.

While the whistle on the roof blew and the windows fogged up, the chipman shook the basket of his deep fryer, turned valves, pumped fuel, and dispensed happiness.

2. The Nuns Just before Christmas, nuns of certain orders travelled around the city collecting for the poor. They used a special closed-in sleigh with a tiny curtained window through which they could peek. If you caught a glimpse of the inside as the sisters stepped out, you saw a simple interior with seats upholstered in leather. The sleigh was immaculately kept. The varnished black exterior carried a small shiny brass plate with the name of the order etched on it. The driver, usually an old sacristan, could protect himself from the weather by rolling down canvas side curtains which had little mica windows. In all, it was an austerely handsome rig, rather like the closed black buggies the Amish people in North America use even today.

3. The Knife Sharpener When we heard Gelindo Bertoldi's sleigh bell outside our house, my mother quickly searched for knives and scissors that needed sharpening, for we never knew exactly when he would pass our way again.

More regularly you would see his sleigh stopped in front of the small neighbourhood butcher shops and grocery stores that gave him steady business in those days before supermarkets.

His sleigh was a travelling workshop with a gas heater. I liked to watch him through its large windows and see the sparks fly as he stood over his grinding wheel, sharpening, repairing, making keys. His sleigh often remained in one place for a long time as he worked, so his horse had a particularly close-fitting canvas-covered blanket.

4. The Fruit Pedlar The fruit and vegetable pedlar had a sleigh that looked like a little house. It was homemade but it had a unique charm because of its little windows and its tiny chimney—this little chimney was the perfect target for our snowballs. Empty fruit crates were stacked on the roof and used to light the coal in the Quebec heater inside. The stove was not so much to keep the driver warm (he usually rode outside), but to keep the produce from freezing. The old horse was protected by a homemade blanket and his pail for drinking water hung on the wall of the sleigh. The pedlar carried a small selection of fruit from door to door in a basket to show and take orders.

Most of the fruit pedlars left the raw wood of their wagons to age like an old barn, though a few, I remember, painted theirs railway-station red.

5. The Milk Sleigh Milk sleighs were out on the streets each winter morning long before daylight. It took a very bad snowstorm to block their way. Sometimes they followed the first snowplough up the street.

The milk horse, like the bread horse, knew the run as well as its driver. While the milkman ran up the steps to deliver at one house, the horse was already moving on to the next stop. The company trademark was painted on the sleigh and stencilled or stitched on the horse's blanket.

On very cold mornings the milk froze before we took it inside. A solid white neck stuck up inches above the bottle, the little cardboard lid still perched on top like a hat. It was a poor children's ice cream.

6. The Royal Mail Sleigh The sleigh that did the pickup from mail boxes was a small low tub-type vehicle pulled by a fairly light, fast horse. When the sleigh was full you saw the sacks sticking up on top, just inside the 'fiddle-rail.'

The Royal coat of arms, the gold-leaf lettering, the deep red colour of the sled, the stencilled GR (King at the time) on the canvas covering the horse, made a very impressive sight. So did the uniform of the driver with the badge of a federal employee on his jacket and fur cap. It all made one feel that here was organization and that the mail would always get through.

7. The Baked Bean Sleigh The beautiful baked bean sleigh was all veneer and varnish, painted in browns and ochres with an illustration of a pot of beans on it. And the beans were just as delicious as they looked.

The bean man passed on set days each week. Housewives came down a few icy steps carrying their empty earthenware bean pots, and got in exchange a full pot, sometimes still hot, from an insulated section of the sleigh.

I used to meet the bean man on Lagauchetière Street just as I was trotting home from school for lunch. And whenever I saw him, I would hope he had stopped at my house.

8. The Movers Sleigh Moving heavy machinery over snow and ice required very special sleighs. These were usually great flat-bed sleds with reinforced runners and truck (the runners assembly). They carried block and tackle, planks, jacks, and ropes, and were pulled by as many as four horses, depending on what was being moved.

Heavy draught horses such as Clydes, Belgians, and Percherons were used and it took a good man to handle them. The bells on the double team had a distinctive series of rings and on very cold days the heavy loads made the runners squeak. Then, too, the vapour that arose from the hard-working horses was like a cloud of steam. You could just feel the power in it all.

9. The Grocery Sleigh Nearly every grocery store had horse and sleigh delivery—although small orders would usually be taken care of by a boy after school, using his own sleigh with a box nailed on top.

The grocery sleighs were pulled by small, compact horses measuring not more than 14 hands and called Quebec ponies. The ponies moved at a quick trot, their bells tinkling rapidly and cheerfully. The delivery boy wore an apron, had a pencil stuck behind his ear, and he carried his loads quickly up those winding staircases of Montreal that could sometimes be treacherously slippery.

Just before Easter the ponies were transformed. Decorated all over with beautiful crêpe paper flowers, they seemed to us to have been touched with magic.

10. The Farmer's Sleigh Among the many sleighs that came to the markets in Montreal, my favourite was the traditional farmer's sleigh, handmade by its owner, and with harness so simple, it could usually be repaired on the farm. The horse pulling this sleigh was the same animal that pulled the plough and did all the other farm chores. Its driver always wore a grey winter coat, tied at the waist with his *ceinture fléchée* (or wool belt), woven with his own pattern on the farm. I don't remember ever seeing a driver without the characteristic pipe in his mouth.

11. The Freight Sleigh The CNR freight sleighs were known as flat-bed sleighs, heavy haulers or cartage sleighs. They were painted the railway's regulation colours and they always carried a broom for sweeping the debris after goods were transferred.

The heavy draught horses—Percherons, Clydesdales and sometimes Shires—were well-equipped with sturdy long straw collars and heavy traces. The metal in the harness was all of polished brass, and sleigh bells hung from the breast straps.

The carter himself had his special equipment, a leather apron to protect his clothes, leather puttees for his legs (usually with a pencil tucked in near the knee), and he always had a pipe in his mouth.

Often, whether regulations permitted it or not, a large fierce dog would ride the sleigh with his master. He protected the freight while the driver made deliveries, but he also kept us from ever hitching a ride.

12. **The Brewery Sleigh** Breweries in nearly all countries took great pride in their horses, harnesses and vehicles; their teams of draught horses were well matched and in beautiful condition. Montreal breweries were no exception.

The team I have illustrated here is typical. The well-groomed Percherons originated in France, a cross of ancient Norman and Arab breeds. They were a deep, dappled grey, docile but extremely powerful. The letter 'V' for Victory and its Morse code symbol · · · — in the form of a brass on the horses' flanks dates this particular pair in the early 1940s and reflects Molson's involvement in the war effort.

The scroll-dash, the fittings and the light double runners were so beautiful, it was hard to realize that this sleigh was really a heavy hauler with a big-load capacity.

13. The Epicure Sleigh If any commercial sleigh could be likened to a Rolls Royce, this one was it. The firm of Henry Gatehouse was established in Montreal in 1891 and catered to the carriage trade. In those days before deep-freezing, the highly perishable quality foods Gatehouse sold were very expensive.

So the sleigh that carried them was appropriately elegant. I was very much impressed with it when I was young and saw it making deliveries to the Queen's Hotel. I particularly remember the oval glass on one side of the sleigh which covered a real stuffed hare, a mallard duck and a quail.

The horse was of a particularly fine breed. Its bells, brasses and traces were highly finished, reflecting the quality of the products listed by the sleigh's lettering. Everything about the Henry Gatehouse sleigh was immaculate, polished and sparkling.

14. The Ragman Harry the ragman never needed to call his customers. The sound of his sleigh was different to all the others and there was no mistaking the dull 'clunk, clunk.' Harry had the only horse with cowbells.

He was our favourite person, our sole source of revenue. We passed on old stove lids, lead pipes, empty bottles and old rags—sometimes, I must confess, not so old. But Harry was more honest than the kids he dealt with and he would often tell us to take things back home.

His horse was an old hack, but he did the job and we all loved him. Layers and layers of potato sacks were on his back to keep him comfortable. One day my mother asked me what Harry called his horse, but when I told her she washed out my mouth with soap.

15. The Snow-Removal Sleigh In the 1930s, when unemployment was high, a heavy snowfall was welcomed, for it meant work. After a snowstorm, every available sleigh was mobilized and men worked around the clock to make the streets passable.

Horse-drawn ploughs pushed the snow from the roadways into high banks. Then it was shovelled into the sleighs and hauled to an open manhole. There the snow was dumped and carried by underground sewers to the river.

Snow-removal sleighs were crudely made of unpainted boards. The sides were built up to hold as much as possible because the owner was paid by the cubic foot of snow hauled. The capacity of each sleigh was stencilled on its side by an Inspector, and a licence issued.

Snow-removal sleighs were the very best to ride on. They moved very slowly, and the drivers seldom bothered us.

16. The Coal Sleigh The coal sleigh was a common sight. It was rough and sturdy and so was the horse. He moved at a slow pace, and had plenty of time to rest while the coal was loaded and unloaded.

The coal was usually delivered in sacks and for the upstairs flats the coalman had to carry the sacks into the coal shed, often up narrow winding steps. His grimy face had clean patches on it where he had wiped the perspiration (and coal dust) off with his mitt.

Ground-floor flats had a chute through a basement window that emptied into the coalbin there. The chute was often a metal brewery sign discarded by a tavern, and the coalman carried a large shovel on his sleigh specially to keep the coal moving down the chute.

17. The *Star* Sleigh The *Montreal Star* sleighs were loaded in Fortification Lane and the papers were delivered to news-stands throughout the city where they sold for two cents.

18. City of Montreal Inspector The City of Montreal Inspector travelled around in a small black cutter, pulled by a small lightweight horse. The Inspector was usually a dignified-looking civil servant who sometimes wore a raccoon coat and a fur hat. His job was to inspect the streets and water hydrants.

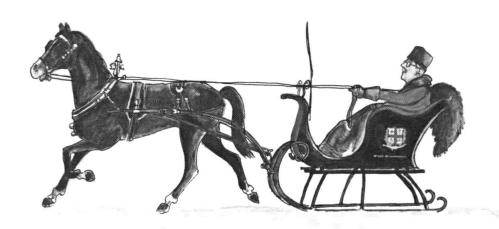

19. The Spice Sleigh The distributor of tea, coffee and spices had his own sleigh. This one had oval side windows, mohair upholstery and many different doors and compartments. To keep the horse from wandering while deliveries were being made, a tie-wait (sometimes called a tie-weight) was attached to his bridle.

20. The Bread Sleigh The daily bread was delivered to the house by horse and sleigh. What I liked best about this sleigh was the little folding step in the rear which made a convenient seat for us to steal rides on.

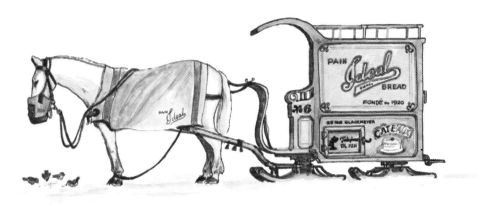

21. The Fire-Hose Sleigh In winter the Montreal Fire Department used highly specialized sleighs often converted from wagons. Here I have painted a drum-type hose sleigh.

I felt very lucky if I was near Station No. 4 at Chaboillez Square when the fire alarm rang and I could see the engines set out. Everything was kept at the ready. The tongue (also known as a pole) of the sleigh—that long single shaft of wood that separates the two horses in a team—with harness affixed and open at the cinches was suspended from the ceiling in the firehouse. At the sound of the alarm the horses had been trained to position themselves under the harnesses. The tongue was then lowered and the cinch straps tightened.

The sleighs, which stood on metal rollers or on greased slide plates recessed in the floor, would then literally explode out of the station.

22. The Fire-Steamer Sleigh This steam-driven pump, its chimney belching smoke and sending sparks flying, was an awesome sight as it raced towards a fire, pulled by three or four horses (sometimes matched greys). Only fire horses were allowed to move at full gallop through the city.

Once at the scene of the fire, these splendid animals were unhitched and led off to a safe place. If the fire station was close enough, they would be taken back there. If not, the firemen would hitch them to a pole out of harm's way.

It was always exciting watching the horse-drawn fire engines, but somehow it was especially so in winter with the red engines against the white snow, the horses blowing into the cold and the bells drowning out all other sounds.

23. The Sightseeing Sleigh Of all the wonderful sleighs that once filled the streets of Montreal, the sightseeing sleigh is the only one still in use. You will find it only on the winding roads of Mount Royal Mountain where no cars are allowed. There all winter long it takes passengers up to the Lookout for a view of the city by day or night.

Today the sleighs are rarely pulled by more than one horse, but I can remember a time when teams of horses were used. The sleighs were bright red, green or blue, had shiny rails and handholds, and carried buffalo robes or bearskins to keep the passengers warm and snug.

But one thing hasn't changed. A ride up Mount Royal by sleigh is still one of the happiest things to do in Montreal during winter.

Carlo Italiano was born in 1920 on a street in Old Montreal that was ideal for sleigh watching and he started drawing sleighs and horses as soon as he could hold a pencil. He grew up to become one of Canada's most popular illustrators. He attended Montreal's Ecole des Beaux-Arts and after World War II joined the staff of the Montreal *Standard*. Since then he has drawn and painted for many magazines and books.

1974 Metropolitan New York Printers' Award for design and printing quality
1975 Canadian Association of Children's Librarians' Gold Medal—Best Illustrated
   Book of the Year
1975 Chosen by Toronto Public Libraries as one of the Top 100 Canadian Children's
   Books
1976 Hans Christian Andersen Honor Award, Athens, Greece

"The technology that gave us the internal combustion engine, diesel buses and mini-bikes also robbed us of sleighs, whose gentle bells were once the most reassuring sound of winter.

Carlo Italiano, a Montreal-born newspaper and magazine illustrator, remembers them and has produced a book that is a magnificent repository of his childhood romance with sleighs. He has written about, sketched and painted them.

In the 1920s and 30s Montreal—not just Montreal but all Quebec—abounded in horse-drawn sleighs. Their tintinnabulations rank with steam locomotive whistles as the most unforgettable sounds of the childhoods they graced. Sleigh bells ornamented perfectly the muteness of deep snow—and Montreal 30 years ago and more was a place where the snow piled up in banks so high they walled in streets, leaving only narrow passages for sleighs.

Sleighs delivered everything: milk, bread, beer, coal, newspapers, groceries, mail. I remember best the high-sided snow carts or tombereaux. Carts and horses formed plodding caravans after every heavy snowfall, carrying snow from the streets to snow dumps on the frozen river.

The snow carts were among the last sleighs to disappear. Some were used through the Second World War, when military priorities slowed the transition from sleighs to trucks.

Though the book's charm crystallizes in Italiano's color paintings, the entire work—and it was plainly a labor of love—is a delight. Bravo, Italiano, who will surely never be found on a snowmobile."
                                                    —London Evening Free Press, Ontario, Canada